i

Nothing More Than Feelings
By
Cherrel
Turner-Callwood

Nothing More Than Feelings

Cherrel Turner-Callwood

ISBN: 978-0-9977601-2-5

Skinulicious Services Publishing

Clearwater, Florida 33760

United States of America

About this author

Author Cherrel Turner-Callwood has always enjoyed writing.

I love the ability to put my thoughts and ideas on paper.

Whether I am writing for adults or children, I get pleasure

knowing that others enjoy reading my work. I look forward

to publishing more work!

Author Cherrel Turner-Callwood enjoys dancing, traveling,

making jewelry as well as being an herbalist and many other

things. She is currently enjoying retired life on the beaches of

Florida.

She can be reached at: skinulicious1@gmail.com

Other Published Books by This Author

The Journey of An Invisible Brown Girl

Children's Books

The Adventures of Chocolate Sunshine

When History Was Black: African Kings and Queens

When History Was Black II: The Making of the United States of America

This is a collection of poetry that I wrote from 1994 through 2001. It is amazing the things you feel when you go through life and learn that writing is your best friend. It is even more amazing that some thoughts apply to our current lives. Many of you can relate to these feelings. Afterall, feelings are real!

Explicit Material! For Adults Only! *

*Any similarities to any situations, events and places are probably real! *

Contents

x

Chapter One

Interesting Feelings

Looking Out My Window

As I sit, looking out my window

I think of the times

that are now like a shadow

I think of the trends

how difficult, how unreal, how complicated

things must have been

For a child to learn at an early age

how terrible things will be

Only to grow to a mature stage

to learn how things will stay

How we live day to day

behind happy faces

while losing our health and our minds

trying to put our true feelings in their places

These things I think of, as I look out my window

Why Should I Hide

Why should I

keep my feelings inside

Being honest and truthful

why should I hide

If one is accepted for who they are

why should I pretend

when my mind is a far

Because you pretend and bend to make a friend

why should I lie or hide

to keep my true feelings inside.

Why try to make me lose my mind

Or better yet, why should I hide

<u>Who Am I Angry With</u>

When the sun does not shine

 who am I angry with

When I am not doing fine

who am I angry with

When society treats me like dirt

who am I angry with

When my husband does not realize my hurt

who am I angry with

When people do not give to me

who am I angry with

When I try to find a way to be free

who am I angry with

When I feel like I am being used

who am I angry with

When as a child, I was abused

who am I angry with

I want to be alone

All my life

I was alone

no parents to love me

no place to call home

no one to worry

no one to care

if I was alive

or if I was not there

I married to fill the lonely hole

Only to find myself lonelier than before

I spend more time alone

my poor soul

I guess I am mad because what did I get married for

I want to be alone

Tragic

There is something I am trying to figure out

Why does it hurt me so

when some people die

People I did not even know

Especially if it was tragic

It really burns inside

I guess because it did not have to be that way

That person did not have to die

You try to live your life

in your own unique way

Someone did not agree with you

so, they decide to kill you today

Why does it affect me

Why do I feel it so

Why does my heart ache

You were someone I wanted to know

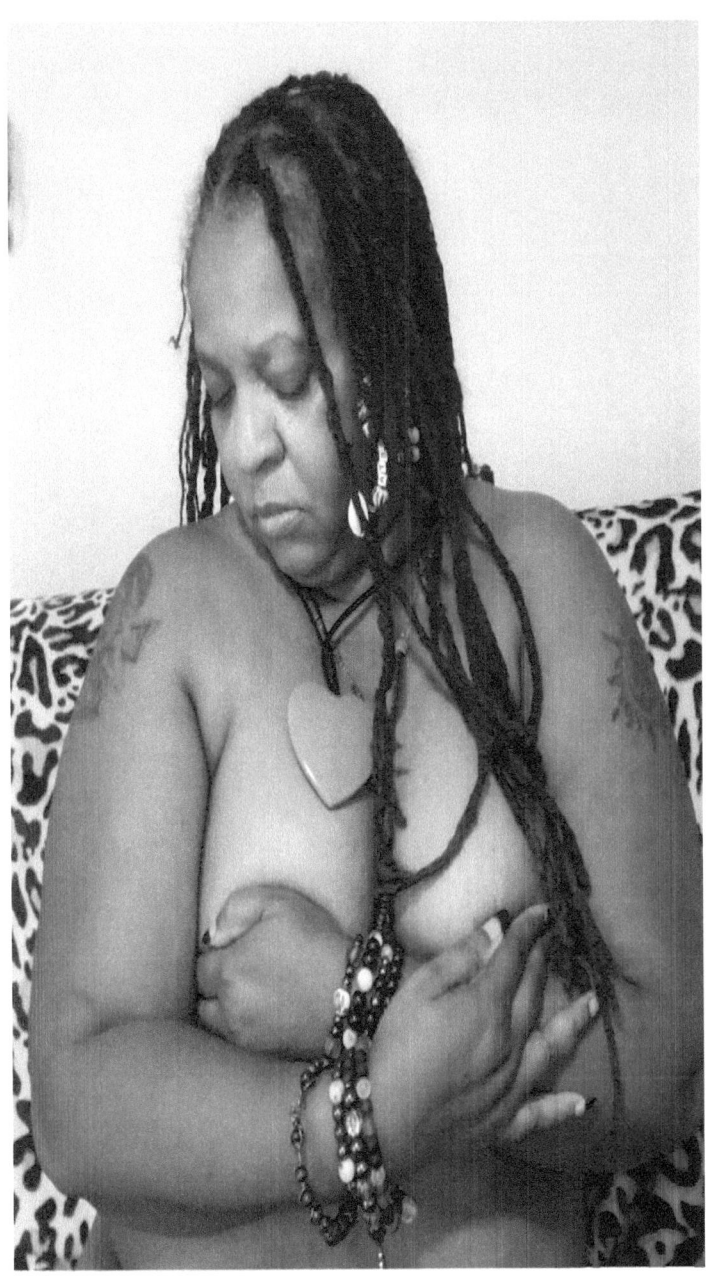

CHAPTER TWO

CHILD SEXUALLY ABUSED FEELINGS

The Tears of a Child

To be born into this world

so innocent so pure

A bouncing baby boy or a girl

To be delivered to parents so unsure

The tears of a child

Wanting the attention and the love

The kisses and the hugs

That God had promised us from above

Only to be pushed and shoved

The tears of a child

To be beat and punched kicked and slapped

Accepting this abuse as a way of life

Learning to hate and to fight back

Being touched and fondled by a father who

did not care for my life

The tears of a child

Searching for love in all places

Clubs jobs family spouse

looking for someone to fill empty spaces

Feeling threaten and like a mouse

The tears of a child

Growing up to be an adult

with so much love to give

Trying to hold on to faith and dreams with results

just so I can go on with my life

so, I can live

The tears of a child

God is so good

God is so real

He gives me the love I need

God is helping me to heal

When I am hungry for love I will not be afraid to feed

The tears of a child

Jesus Loves Me

Jesus loves me

yes, I know

Why did He allow

my father to touch me so.

Why did he allow

A child so young

to be molested by a man

so full of cum

How does Jesus expect me

to honor a father

who did not respect me

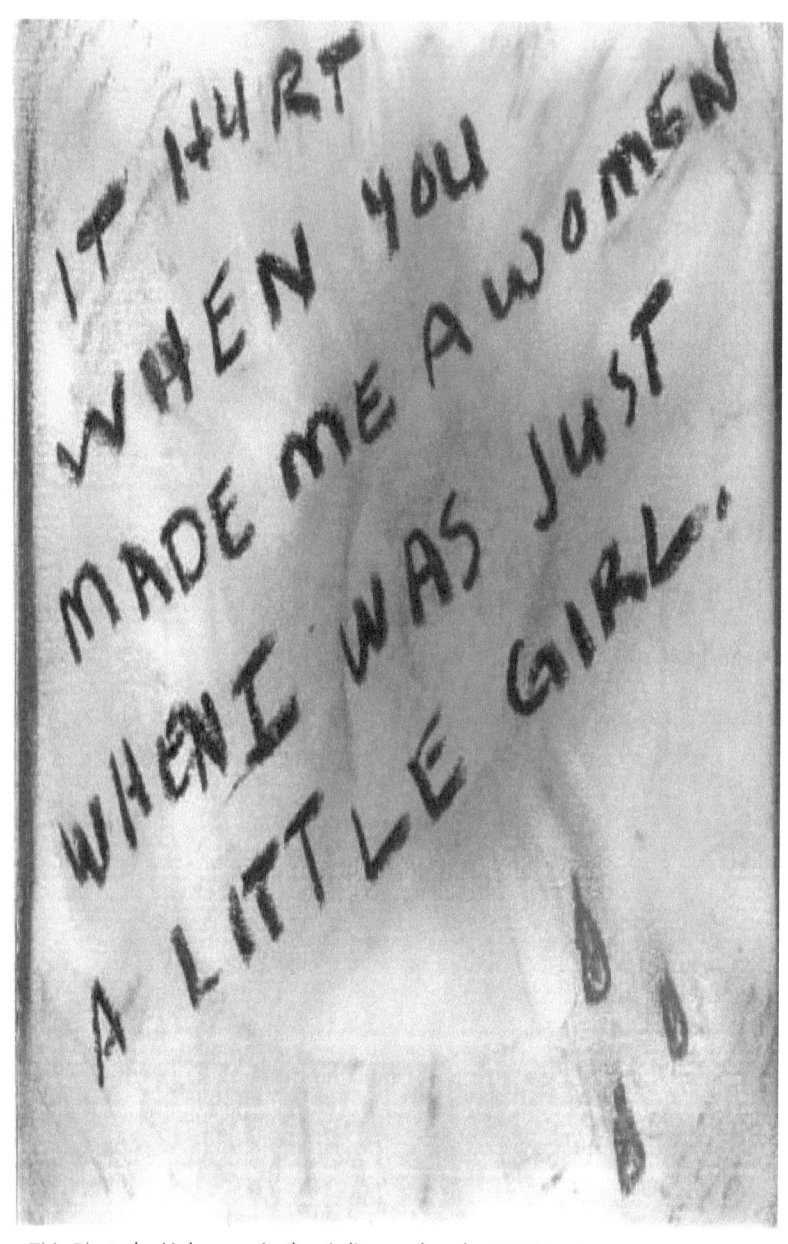

It Had to Happen to Me

Why did it happen to me

Why was I punished so

I cannot seem to get a grip on things

no matter how much I know

The holidays are arising

I feel so much anger and so much pain

because the man who is my father

had so much more to gain

Does he realize how he has destroyed me

How bitter he has made me

Because he claimed he was drunk

when he screwed me.

When he said he was drunk

but forgot when he was sober

when I was in the kitchen

and my stepmother on the sofa

How he would threaten and scare me

as he put his fingers in my pants

He said I would not live to be sixteen

if I told my aunt.

How he got so much pleasure

by causing me pain

He even told his friends

at the bar Jollies in the rain

Now every Christmas

and every New Year

I feel hurt, angry, sorrow and grief

because he took away my childhood years

Damaged Rhyme

 Mother Goose

Donald Duck

my stepmother got drunk

as I got fucked

She did not care

that I was ruined for life

She did not care about my tears

She just wanted to be his wife

Just put her on punishment

or kick her out the house

She is not worth the argument

she does not hold any power

How can people act like they did not know?

that a child never had a life?

Instead of protecting her, treating her like a whoc

When her father did things, he did to his wife

O Christmas Tree

O Christmas tree

O Christmas tree

How lovely are thy branches

O Christmas tree

O Christmas tree

he touched me every chances

You still so green

with flashing lights

While he screwed

me in the night

O Christmas tree

O Christmas tree

how lovely are thy branches

Untitled

Twinkle twinkle little star

How I wonder where you are

Shining through the night so bright

While my father screwed me in the night

Twinkle twinkle little star

How I wonder where you are

Nursery Thyme

One two he looked at you

Three four he shut the door

Five six he rubbed his prick

Seven eight he laid me straight

Nine ten he stuck it in

Eleven twelve he is going to Hell

Thirteen fourteen I was barely a teen

Fifteen sixteen he took advantage of me

Seventeen eighteen he was always waiting

Nineteen twenty I am in misery

Repeater

He said it would not happen again

it was all a mistake

To try to make me into a woman

even though it was not his place.

To remind me of the purpose

for me being born on this earth

Created to serve his purpose

not having any worth

I will not do it again

I was drunk

Suppose to be my father, a man

instead, some type of punk

He said he would not do it again

I tell you it was a lie

He finally succeeded in my teens

when I developed a behind

How dare you stick your fingers in my pants

with her in the other room

You were not checking the water in the plants

nor were you my groom

P A T

Pain and agony

tears and defeat

touching me all over

as though I was a piece of meat

Abandonment and abuse

drunk and unstable

threats and misuse

being forced on a table

How could you be so wrapped up in yourself

ignoring the cries, warnings and clues

why did not you act like a mother without a doubt

 protecting your child who was a gift to you

Chapter Three

Challenging Feelings

In the Company of Yours

You do not have to grit on me

I am not trying to take your place

I just want to enjoy your presence

not to space

in the company of yours

they say there is strength in numbers

there is even more among friends

I just want to get to know you

so, we can join in

in the company of yours

I am not your competition

I am not trying to put you out

I only want to share with you

to find out what you are about

in the company of yours

it is tough being a woman

in today's fast pace

but we must worry about color

in this world of hate

in the company of yours

So, you see sister

I need to be in tune to you

But I wonder if you realize

You need to be in tune to me too

Neighbor of Mine

I saw him coming through your window

in the daylight when you were alone

I decide to come meet you I had to stop his show

So, I went first to use the phone

I notice his car riding by

our neighborhood throughout the week

Of course, he did not notice the eyes

that were looking after the weak

I cut your hedges just the other day

I thought they had grown too high

I did not want them in the way

Of my neighborhood eye

I noticed that you did not have any lights

On the outside of your home

I put a few in that were bright

so, I can see your house even when you were gone

Why would you do this for me

Why would you care

I did not even think you noticed me

way over there

I believe in love, peace and tenderness

I also believe in looking out for each other and being kind

That is why I could not do anything less for you

neighbor of mine

Chapter Four

Spiritual Feelings

How I Love Thee

Lord I love you so much

It is a love I would never feel

no matter how much I want to

I would never find a love so real

there is nothing in his world

that could equal to your love

you give it so freely

right from the Heavens above

and you share it with so many

this is hard to believe

you love me without wanting anything

just for me to believe in your Son indeed

you love me as I am

changes things I cannot see

you know I am unique

that is the way you want me to be

you do not hang your love over me

like a weight when I make a mistake

you do not hold it against me

when I arrive too late

you love me when I do not love myself

you never hate

Heavenly Streams from Afar

What a beautiful time it will be

when the Heaven doors open

and come down for all to see

When God and His angels take their seats

bringing a new home for His people to be

How clean and pure and full of color

not for just one race, culture, creed or color

What a site that will be

When Jesus Christ takes His seat

the sinless man who died for our sins

He loves us so much

without him we cannot win

The ticket is paid for

the price is free

Without Jesus in your life

God's face you will not see

Reading Soothes the Soul

God give us all the tools

we need in life

whether it is a struggle or

whether it is a flight

You and I have the ability

to be whatever we want in the Universe

Whether we are near or whether we are far

reading is the answer to be who we are

In order to advance or to succeed

the key to it all is the ability to read

Who Loves You Babe

Loving God seems so hard

with too many strings attached

It is like reading Hallmark cards

with love, dreams, thoughts you cannot match

He loves us unconditionally

for the Bible says so

But when we trip and skin our knee

God does not love us; is this so

What is a person to do or to think

when they are hurting and feel pain

when they are not sure what to say or to blink

because others say they complain

Loving God is not that hard you know

for as the Bible says

God loves you from the day you are born

and until your dying day!

Congratulations

Congratulations on your engagement

as you can see

God blesses all His children

even you and me

Our lives are like storybooks

waiting to be told

Each one is different

made into a unique mold

Everyone needs to be loved

by one that is picked for us

God made these choices from above

and I am sure he made a big fuss

Enjoy your lives together

putting God first

You would never need anything

because he will quench your every thirst

Don't Judge A Book by Its Cover

People make it hard

to be loved by God

They convince you to lead a better life

do not make a mistake or nod

Then they chop you up with a knife

I guess the reason I am getting sick

is because the pain I feel

When I do not fit into the clique

of people who cannot deal

Those who tend to feel

they are holier than thou,

When one stumbles or slip

Then try to convince themselves it is allowed

when it is their turn to trip

I wonder how these people would feel

when they finally see

That they do not really fit the bill

they are no better than you or me

So, do not judge a book by its cover

this is not a good deed

Because when you judge another

you will be judged even harder indeed

Chapter Five

Feminine Feelings

You Question

You question my being a wife

when I wanted my feelings respected

when the man in my life

wants me to do what he expected

You question my womanhood

for my decision to stay at home

I do things you only wish you could

so, you try to make me feel like I am alone

You question my mothering

when I want to teach and watch my children grow

you say I am smothering them

but you are not home with yours so what do you know

You are questioning my sexuality

when I tell my man no

it is not my fault he cannot accept reality

when he does not treat me right, I am not his whoe

Before you think about questioning me

telling me what I should and should not do

check yourself because you see

just as you question me someone is questioning you

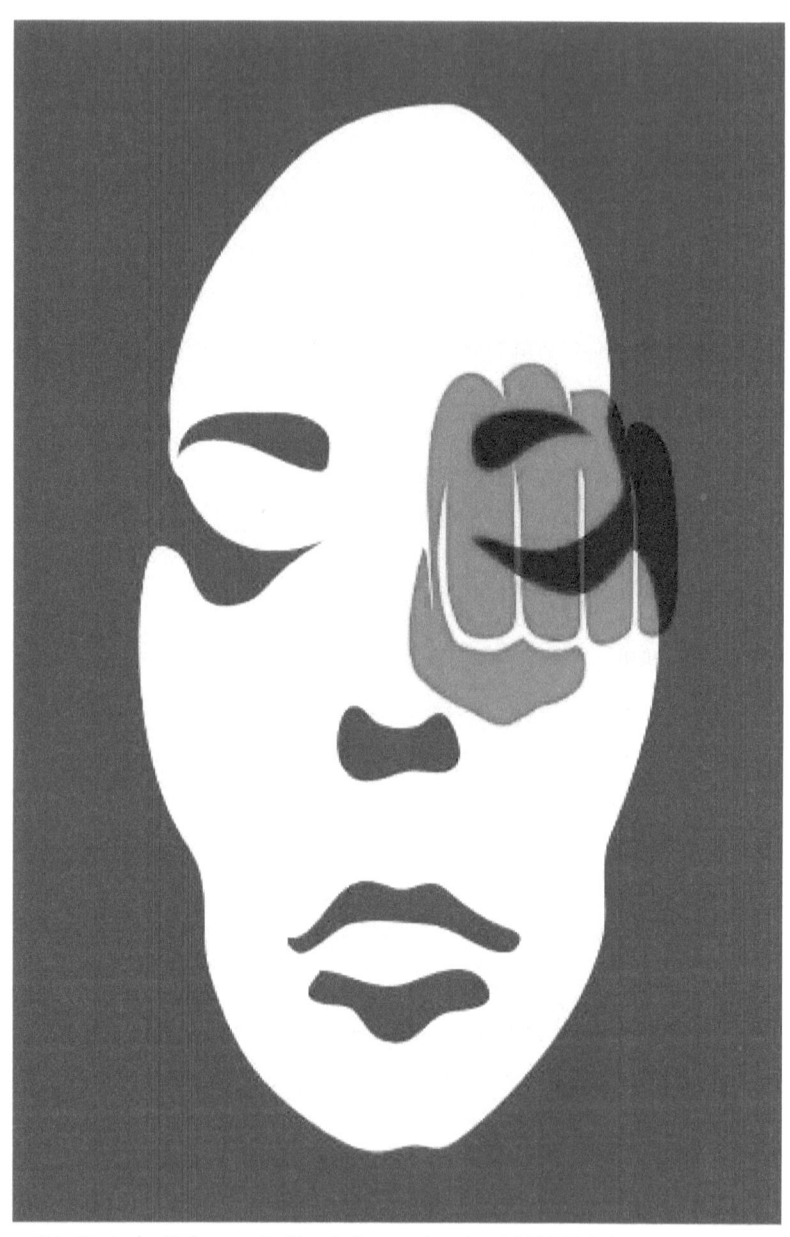

Unfelt Fear

The fear these women must have felt

as they live day to day

When the men in their lives

could not have their way

The pain they tried to resist

for whatever reason they must

Every time that man lifts his fists

the man they trust

The tearing of their hearts

when they tried to reach out

To a world that defends other parts

leaving an abused woman to protect herself

Unfair Rights

What gives one the right

when a woman makes a mistake

Of loving and trusting a man she thought right

who quickly realizes when he punched her in the face

Who uses his size, his strength and power

to control every part of herself

To do and say things every hour

so, she would be too scared to get help

Help which is extremely hard to find

from people who do not believe

That she is physically, verbally and emotionally abused

could not take it anymore so she wanted to leave

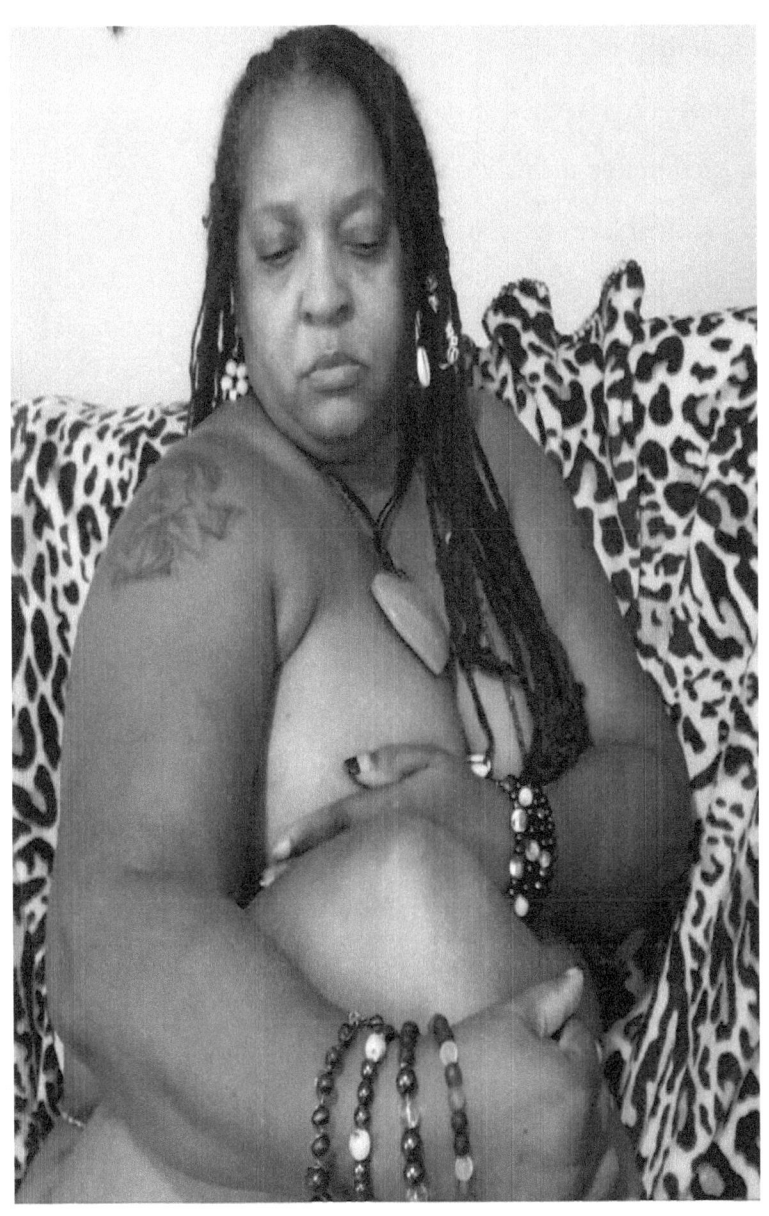

Emotional

The hurt that I feel

as I think of the women

Who tried to live their lives for real

who lost their lives to men

The anger I feel

when every day I awake

To see how people, continue to treat

women who are abused by their mates

It makes me distrust every man

I cannot sleep at night

wondering how long I will live

So, my sons will be taught this is not right

Who is to Blame

We blame women

when they kill their mates

No one will help them prevent the attacks

they did not plan it nor was it hate

When they defended themselves

when society turned its back

This cycle must be broken

everyone must learn

Women are human beings and often soft spoken

not something you slap, punch, threaten, trap or burn

Woman at Home

You can talk down about me

because I chose to stay home

You said I was nothing

you said I was no one

If I do not work to bring a paycheck home

I could not possibly be doing anything

sitting at home

Some of us must work

we have no man at home

Some of us are independent

we like having our own

There is no reason

why a woman cannot work

But she takes good care of your kids

even though you treat her like dirt

You need to respect

the woman who chooses to care for her children

While you were busy

trying to prove yourself to society

that you are worth as much as men

A woman at home is not less of a woman

she has feelings just like you

The only difference of a working woman

at home women do not get paid for the job they do

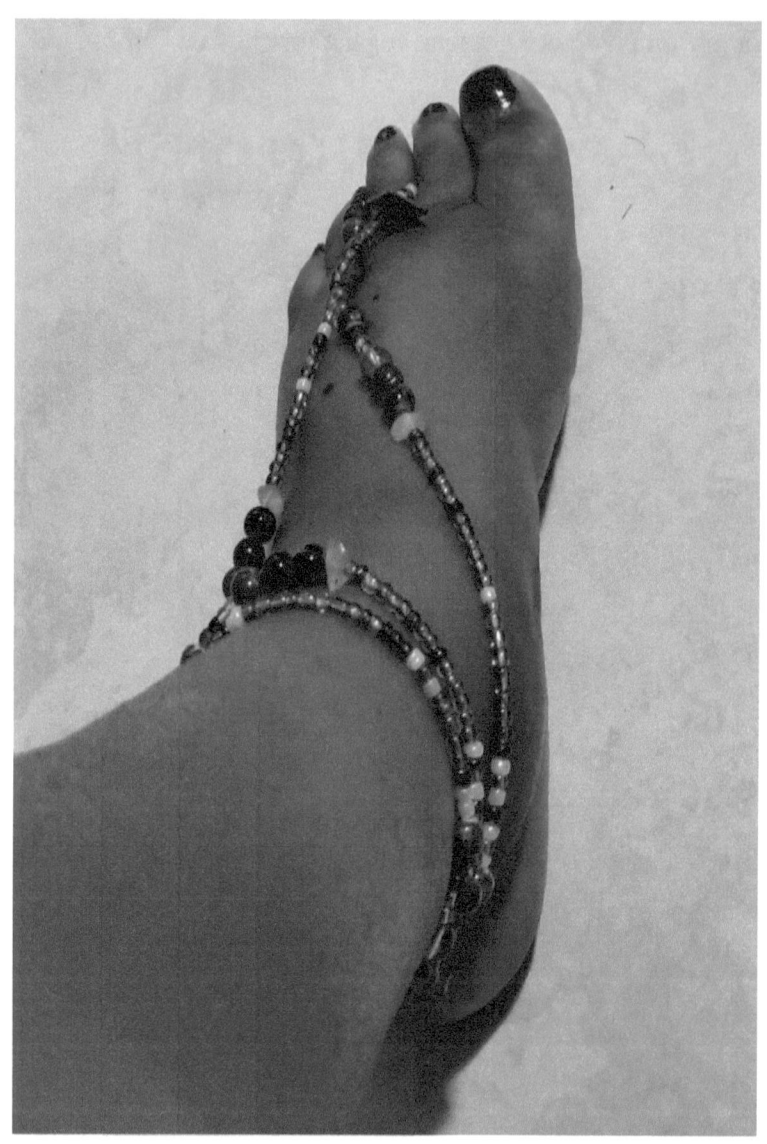

Get Well

When you feel under the weather

and I have not seen you for a day or two

Remember in my heart we are together

Feel better soon and I love you

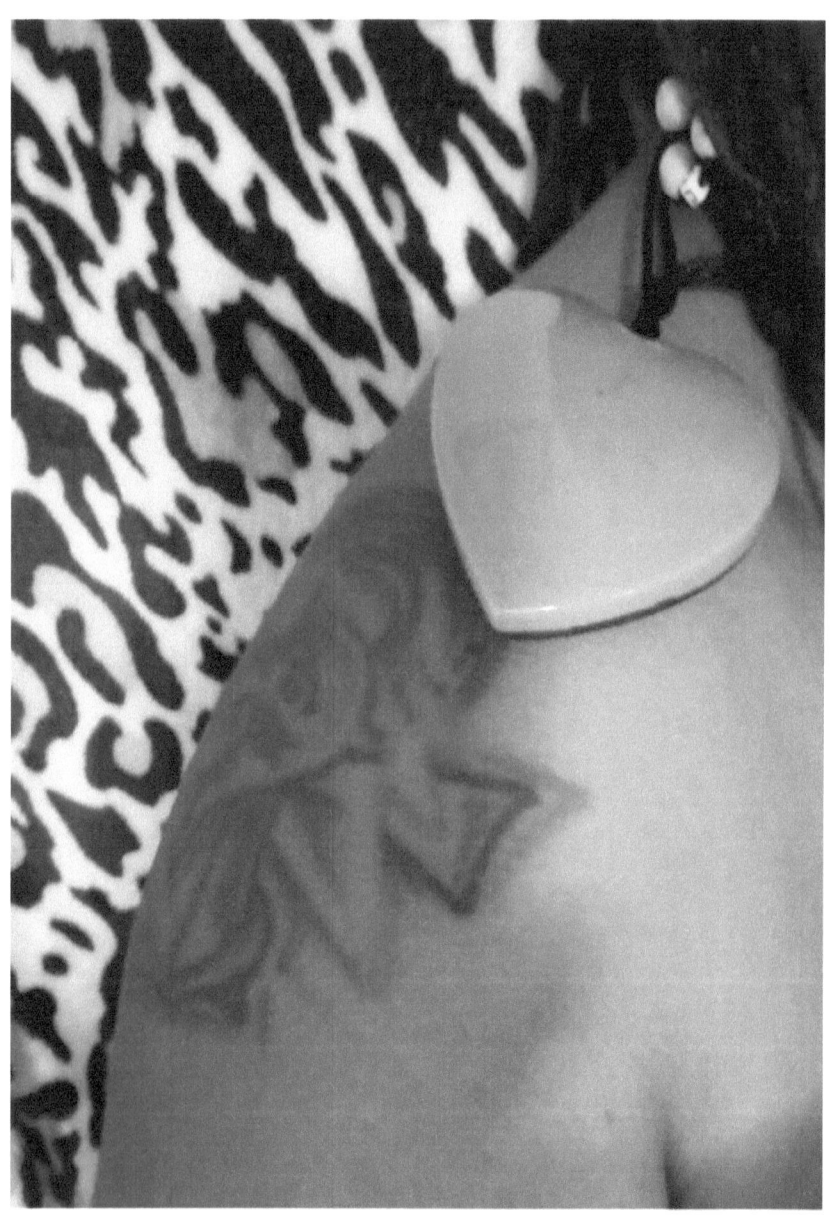

Chapter Six

Heart Felt Feelings

To You

You said you loved me

you said you cared

but when I needed you

you were not there

You could not be content with me

I was not enough flame or was I just a fad

I changed that, I was more than enough

there were just others you had to have

You said I was a cry baby

when my feelings were hurt

what difference did it make to you

To you I was less than dirt

What have I done to you

for you to treat me this way

All I ever wanted was for you to be true

You did not care, you just wanted to play

You leave me in tears

Why do you hate me so

Am I paying for the years

others had you blow

I cannot sleep and eat

All I do is cry

But I get over this

As for now, my heart just died

In the Company of Yours

Lost and confused

You think I do not notice

the things you say and do

you do not think I am aware

of all the things you keep to you

You act like you do not understand

when I think you are out to get me

this has been going on for eight years

it is not something I just want to be

God must have something powerful in store

for the changes I go through

I am better than this, I deserve much more

when I leave, what will you do

Thoughtless

Do you ever wonder

where you would be

if you had just been honest

to one who believe in loyalty

Do you even realize how much I hurt

Maybe you really do not care

How silly I must have been to plan

my life and future with you

Telling you my plans about us

the things I want us to do

What I would have done because of you

And the love I had for you

You knew all along you were not interested in me

You made life for me, loving you

as difficult as can be

Why did you place me on hold

Why do you lie to me

I could have been over this

If you had of just let me be

See-Saw Burnt Heart

You crushed my heart

make the pain stop

Fed me all types of untrue stories

continued to mess around

Pretend to be interested in me and my sons

ended my four-and-a-half-year friendship

Made me cry

What have I ever done to you

Had me wait for you

Isolated me

and brought me back to the beginning within a year

all in the best interest of you

Building your life around someone else

life is too short for games and loneliness

Why do you hate me so

We should be progressing

instead of reverting backwards

what am I waiting for

boy do I feel cheated again

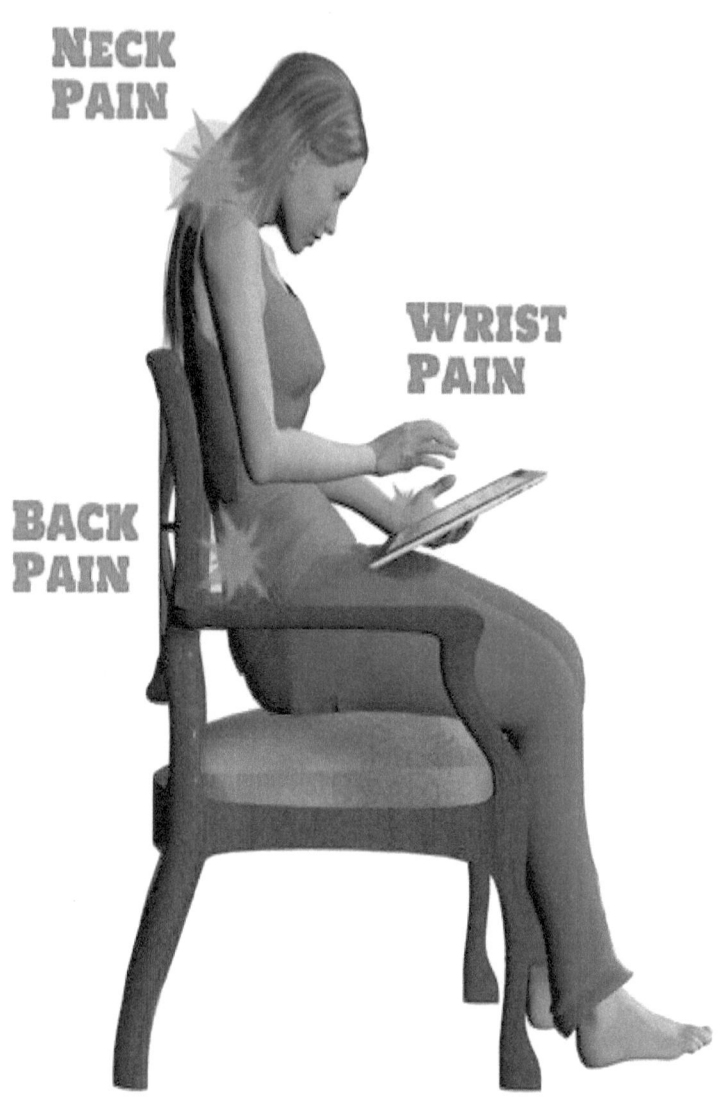

NECK PAIN

WRIST PAIN

BACK PAIN

How My Body Hurts

Head, I have continuous headaches

my thoughts are cluttered

all I want to do is sleep

I cannot believe this is happening to me

My Eyes hurt from the things I see

they hurt from the tears that continued to fall

they hurt from the tears that will not fall

My Face burns with embarrassment

the shame I feel for allowing someone to hurt me

I wonder if I did not have any children

what would I do with this situation?

My Ears deceive me of the things I want to hear

but do not hear

My Mind ignores the truth

I have a mind freeze

My Mouth from the lack of smiling

 and the words that are left undone

 since there are no happy thoughts

there is no such use for a smile

My Throat for the lump that

 remains stuck there

There is tension in my <u>Neck</u> for

trying to keep my head up

despite of how I feel

My <u>Chest</u> which is finding it difficult to breathe

It feels like someone has put their full weight on my chest

My <u>Heart</u> continues to hurt

it is like the knife was inserted and

when the person decided to make me feel the full effect

it was sat on and went right through my <u>Back</u>

it hurts REAL BAD

Insecure

How stupid could I be

to believe what you say

Even though I knew you lied to me

I really wanted to believe

the things you say

when the truth is you wanted to do

whatever you wanted to do

I feel dumb to sit on the side

to try to convince myself that you love me

when I know deep down inside you do not

you must see me as slut

While you cater to your future

because you know I am not a health risk

while you wait for your day to come

I wish you the best in life

I am glad your dreams are coming true

you deserve the good things in life

it is just sad that my heart had to pay the price

But I will not pay for no one else

Sharing

Of all the things I shared with you

the things of my heart

Once you had the things you wanted

you decide to insert the knife

You turned it every which way you could

pulled it out

then inserted again

I always will remember that life is cruel

I thought I really knew until now

The things you take me to

are all about you

Nothing is about me

I wonder how long it would take

for me to get over you

My hats go off to you

for a job well done

I feel like a fool

Whew

Is it love or exhaustion

that makes a person stay

In a relationship that makes them question

what will happen today

Maybe it is pride

because who likes to fail

When you think you gave a free ride

instead of enjoying the sail

Maybe it is fantasy

of things you dream will come.

Then the thing called reality kicks in

then you feel dumb

Should there be a price for happiness and peace

does everyone have a price

One person holds the leash

the other one a grain of rice

The Clock Is Running Out

The Clock is running out

Soon you will be on the road

trying to figure out

why you decided not to let go

It feels good just to be me

not having to worry about the kids

Oh yeah and that husband of mine

he says that he loves me

but treats me so wrong

He cannot make me happy

His clock is running out

Just do not know what I am going to do

maybe I will just leave with the kids

and never come back

maybe I will come back for a while

then leave and never come back

I could just forget about men altogether

and just think of me and my kids

I do not need a man to satisfy me

they just do not understand

The Clock is running out

They do not know how to talk to me

and surely do not know how to make love to me

I am tired of this man going off the deep end

he always has some reason or excuse

he says he is my friend

he needs to take responsibility for his actions

Man his clock is running out

I cannot take it anymore

if I had the money, I would leave

he is no good for me he causes me grief

I was doing so much better before I met him

I really do not need him he makes me sick

I would never forget the things he done to me

I would never forgive

His clock is running out

I do not have time to wait for this child

to become a man

His clock is running out

Who Can I Turn To

Who can I turn to

when I am feeling down and low

Who can I turn to

when I have no place to go

Who can I turn to

when I am tired and confused

Who can I turn to

when I feel I am going to blow my fuse

No one should have to spend so much time alone

Everyone needs someone they can rely on

It hurts to know I cannot get on the phone

and that my only relief is by writing a poem

I cannot turn to my parents

I would not dare

They were never there for me

They do not care

My other relatives never cared about me

only if I came around bringing them treats

I cannot turn to my husband

I must be nuts

He is another reason why I do not trust

No one understands

my hurts and my pain

All I always hear

is that I am to blame

I am always there when

someone needed me

even you

can you tell me

Who can I turn to

www.ingramcontent.com/pod-product-compliance
Lightning Source LLC
Chambersburg PA
CBHW021936170626
46807CB00007B/3131